Y'all
JUST DON'T
Know

Y'all JUST DON'T Know

Published by Krystal Lee Enterprises (KLE Publishing)
Copyright © 2025 by Lacosha Johnson. All rights reserved. Please send comments and questions:

Krystal Lee Enterprises
770-240-0089 Ext. 1
sales@KLEPub.com

To Reach the Author:
Email: me@lacoshajohnson.com

Web: LacoshaJohnson.com
Social Media All Channels: @LacoshaJohnson

Printed in the United States of America.
All rights reserved. No part of this book may be reproduced or transmitted in any form or by any means, electronic or mechanical, including photocopying, recording, or any information storage and retrieval system without written permission of the publisher except for brief quotations used in reviews, written specifically for inclusion in a newspaper, blog, magazine, or academic paper.

ISBN: 978-1-945066-80-1

Dedication

I dedicate this book to people who were born to unusual circumstances, who faced many challenges, and who determined to win anyhow; this book is for you.

Acknowledgment

I would like to express my sincere appreciation to Felix for his unwavering support in achieving the success of my first book. To my children, I convey my deepest love and hope that this book provides a valuable life lesson. Additionally, I would like to thank Lynn and Lace Photography, Loc Elegance, and Divine Enhancement for their contributions to the photo cover.

Y'all Just Don't Know

Table of Contents

Introduction	7
Chapter One	11
Chapter Two	15
Chapter Three	23
Chapter Four	37
Chapter Five	51
Chapter Six	65
Chapter Seven	77
About the Author	89

Introduction

I know people promise that their books are going to be great, but they can be lackluster. I promise you this book will not be that. I was born to extremely young parents, and yes, I had to learn life through their mistakes and youth. Things that should have never happened, arguably did; however, I am grateful for it all.

It wasn't all bad, though. I had a family much larger than my parents, and that was what saved me in the long run. I was born in the South, and that says a lot you should know before we begin in a small town of Covington, GA.

Although my parents were very smart, they didn't have an in-depth education. My mom's education was cut short, while on the other hand, my dad's life was cut short. I was the first of my grandmother Shirley's bloodline to obtain a college degree.

They were born at a different time when hard work was more valuable than education. Perhaps that was some sense of failure to most; the family valued work and not education. Many of my family members had hearts and wisdom bigger than any education you could obtain.

My Parents, of course, weren't able to provide for me in any significant way. They were children trying to find their own path, but were not mature enough for a child. If both Mom and Dad had not made the brave decision of letting me reside with my Great-Aunt, who knows what my story would be? This is why I must share it!

I was led to write this book because I believe in breaking generational curses. My mom was a teen mom. I am glad to say that I was not. My mom's story is not my story, but she paved the way for me to have a story to tell you. My parents struggled to manage life. I am stable, and while my family dynamic is still a bit different than the traditional ways, it is nothing like mine when I was growing up.

I am grateful for my Aunt and Uncle who jumped in to help raise me. I refuse to allow the circumstances of my youth to hold me back from believing in pushing for what I desire. I refused to shun my beginning but saw how I could make good out of an unusual situation.

I cannot judge my parents' decisions or their youth, because they could have chosen to abort me, but they decided to take the hard road of having a child while still being children. I could have been the story that never manifested or lived long enough to tell. But I am here, and so are you.

If you want to be encouraged by a story of a survivor, you have found it. If you need to see the light at the end of the tunnel, I am here to blaze a way forward for you. I will share my truth to help you or someone you know avoid and correct mistakes that you may have experienced in life. Perhaps this may even help you to understand unusual circumstances and help a child who feels lost and incomplete.

Turn the pages with me and see glimpses of my life that may mirror yours and allow me to show you how I overcame, and others can too.

Lacosha Johnson

Chapter ONE

My mother and father were from the same neighborhood, "Jamestown." My dad was originally from Monticello, GA, and at some point in his life, moved to Covington, GA "Jamestown," but my mother was born and raised here. You know the city that is just past Conyers and is becoming a mecca for production companies and new businesses today, that's it. My parents met through my aunt and uncle, who helped them raise me. My dad worked with my uncle at Bulldog Tire Company and would often visit my uncle and aunt, where he met my mom.

When I was growing up, and even during the time of my mother coming up, it was a small country town. Everyone knew each other and to a large extent each other's business. We were aware of our family lines and who belonged to a "good family."

I know you have heard about big families, but I have a really large, close family. I mean, I have about 20 plus biological uncles and aunts between my two parents. Before you ask, this was a different time, and yes, having children was the norm. Culturally, we were born during a time when breeding wasn't too far in the past. When you ain't got much to do, I mean outside of connecting with family, I guess making children was a pastime. Just what exactly were people to do for recreation, fun, to feel loved, and build families? At least that is what it seemed like back in the day.

My grandparents were vital to our society and community. The town knew their names, and they were welcomed. All of my grandparents' children went on to have lots more children and further our legacy. I am proud of where I come from and grateful for my parents' roots.

Both of my parents were raised with decency, order, and belief. My family is big on believing in God. I grew up in church. I attended mostly with my childhood friend and her mother, and being raised by my Aunt and Grandmother, I have the Spirit of God buried deep into my heart. My mother was always a woman who had a mind of her own, while my dad was the total opposite.

Mom didn't listen much to anyone. She was a strong person growing up. She never spanked me for anything, but she could look at you a certain way and hurt your soul. Her discipline was verbal and facial expressions, and she was like that with her siblings. Because she was my grandmother's firstborn and was born to young parents (see the repeated pattern), I think that Shirley (her mom) was a little bit more lenient with her.

Mom was always quick-tempered and wanted what she wanted. She didn't apologize for being who she was, and everyone accepted that. She is a lady with a big personality who was a strong, stubborn, and independent firecracker. She was mature for her age, and she was ahead of others by several years. Maybe my grandmother was also an old soul even then?

My dad was always a quiet and humble person. He loved his mother, and I had always admired the way he looked at my mom. Both of my parents loved their girls. My mom had one other child, and my dad did too. We are all girls who have and have had parents who genuinely love us, despite our circumstances.

It was strange because my mother was always in and out of my grandmother's home. It was a place where all of us could go back to if we couldn't make it on our own. The same rule applied to my father in his mother's home. They both had to follow house rules, which led them to try harder to be on their own.

You know the rule of teenagers, they know best and they judge everything. My family wasn't perfect, and I learned early on that no one is. I don't judge either one of them for the choices they made. That is what love allows you to do: to love people regardless of their shortcomings.

My grandmothers had a unique situation on both sides. My maternal grandmother lived in the house with her mother and her kids. My Paternal grandmother lives in a house beside her mother. This made it fortunate enough for me to know both great-grandparents. My mother's living arrangements weren't very easy because she lived in a home with five other siblings and two cousins.

I recall my maternal grandmother providing for her children and for the community. When someone was hungry, she always made a way to give them a meal. My mother would host block parties, do small events in the yard that would feed everyone, and allow us all to take a break from the complications of life to just have fun. This is what living in "Jamestown" was all about.

My mom was pretty. She was young, but if you talked to her, I am sure her wisdom was far beyond a 14-year-old's mindset. She knew the importance of family and wanted that for herself, too. Now, I am not saying she was out there trying to find Mr. Right to have a baby and get married. My dad always pushed us to have the best chances at life, and that went for my mother, too.

He was the one who pushed education conversations. The idea of a family seems promising until you realize that in your youth, you don't have all the facts. You have the vision, but you don't see all the dots that must connect to help you arrive at it. You assume that not knowing these fine details won't make a big difference, but they make a huge difference.

We had about five streets that made up our community, and on three of those blocks, I had close family ties.

Chapter Two

I am not sure how long my parents dated in private before I came into the picture. What I do know is that they had good hearts toward each other and wanted to do right by me. My mom had me just a few months before she turned 15 years old in 1980. My birth story was eventful.

The pressure hit my mother, and her water broke at home. She was taken to the hospital by her stepdad, her Mom, and her Aunt. On the way to the hospital, the light was shining on her stepdad's bald spot, and this made my mom and aunt laugh, so that my mom wouldn't be so focused on the pain. When they got to the hospital, the ER Nurse took my mom back to prep to have me, and there was a wheelchair outside the door.

My grandmother was extremely tired and sat in the wheelchair. Another nurse came down the hall and thought my grandmother was the pregnant patient and was about to push her in for delivery. It wasn't until my aunt told them, "She's not pregnant. Her daughter is in the room ready to deliver her grandchild."

When it came time for my mom to push, one of

the times she bit my grandmother's hand and wouldn't let go until my aunt made her. My mother said she was in a lot of pain. It's a good thing I was born pretty quickly after arriving at the hospital. My aunt and my grandmother were present for my delivery. My dad was not there because he was at one of his Disc Jockey jobs. However, he did arrive later.

I loved that my family didn't abandon my mother or watch her struggle because of me, her age, and her circumstances. I'm not sure how much I changed her life. I don't know what dreams she might have felt she gave up to be a mother. I often wonder if she had thoughts about not having the time to achieve something she wanted.

I know that for every mother who felt shackled by children, there is another who would say they were her saving grace. I believe that was the case for my parents, and I'm going to tell you why. Things for my parents started off complicated, and they didn't get any less difficult.

From birth, I had a family of mothers and an extended family that served as father figures to me. It was a good thing because my parents were young, making adult decisions. They were trying to figure it out as best as they could, and unfortunately, their marriage was broken.

After I was born, my parents were still dating. My mom and dad got married in 1985, a few years after I was born. My mom was 19 and my dad was 25. They got married because they were in love, and my dad proposed to my mom. They had a pretty good relationship until they separated for irreconcilable differences. They weren't forced by their family to marry, either. And although they separated, they were still married until the day my dad died.

Chapter Two

My mom loved my father since the day she met him. They grew close quickly, and that love she had never ended, although it was strained by the choices they made. When they got married, they didn't buy a house and ride off into the sunset. Our lives parallel each other as we all lived between 2nd and 5th streets, but never together. I stayed on 3rd Street, my mom on 2nd Street, and my dad on 5th Street. They never lived together alone, so it's a miracle how a relationship blossomed into a baby and marriage.

I remember that night when my mom left my dad. The next morning, he looked at me and asked, "Do you want to stay here with me and my mom? Or do you want to stay with your aunt?" I told him that I would like to go with my aunt. My mom was ok with it because my aunt helped my mom out a lot with raising me since I was a baby. She and my grandmother both wanted me to have a stable place to go to school.

I don't blame them for allowing me to go and move in with my aunt. I loved them both, and I often missed my time with my parents, but they never fully went away, either. They were always around and checking on me. They didn't live too far, so I was close to them, although I didn't live with them.

I did hold resentment in my heart toward my mom, if I am honest. In part because I was told she left me. I didn't know all the circumstances, but my heart was in pain cause it bothered me that she would leave me and not take me with her or to my aunt. One day, as a grown woman, I decided to ask my mom, "Mom, why did you leave me?"

I know that was a bold question, but when you're

tired of hurting and want out, you'll overcome your fear of judgment quickly. I wanted–needed answers so I could heal and let this anger or bitterness go in my life. She told me that the night she left, she was intending to leave with me.

The night was dark, cold, and raining. I remember my parents having a disagreement. Although I should have been in bed sleeping, I was up. I couldn't help but try to hear what was going on even though it wasn't my business. Then I went on to sleep.

We were staying at my Dad's Mom's house, and I think this was part of the confusion or strain on their marriage. I do believe he could have gotten help and been better if they had their own place. When I would ask where my mom went the next morning, I remember very clearly him saying to me, "She left us."

My Dad did tell me about my sister, who was just a few months younger than me. He told me everything - his regret and pain - because he was my friend. The only thing he lied to me about was his drug addiction. He was functional and hid it well from me. I came up with my own ideas because I never asked the right questions. I kept my questions in instead of asking. My mother further explained that his mother wouldn't let her take me because it was cold and raining.

She was still a young adult and had a lot of responsibilities if she would have had me with her. She most definitely would have complicated her life more at a time when she, too, was grieving the loss of her marriage. Divorce is a hard thing that I would also become familiar with.

Chapter Two

It wasn't hard to adjust to moving permanently with my aunt and uncle. I absolutely loved it because I was the only girl, and they spoiled me. My great-grandmother and aunt tried to help me understand, forgive, and not hold a grudge against my parents.

My mom learned to forgive, too, and later moved on to her second relationship, where she would have my baby sister some years later. I have to admit, although we didn't all grow up together, we have all seen different versions of our parents. My mom was upset with my father for what he did, but he was her first love.

The two of them, over the years, kept in touch, and probably, if they both hadn't moved on, they could have been together. Later in life, when my mom's other relationship ended, it seemed like a glimmer of hope that the two would get back together.

I remember thinking this was great! Maybe their getting back together could mean I spend the last years of my (middle/high) years with both of them. Growing up and seeing them both come and go, or only spend a few days here and there, began to bother me as I grew older. I wanted to have a normal family setup for me and my sisters, but instead, I learned a lot of dysfunctional ways to cope with my pain from not asking the right questions and understanding the dynamics.

But the most hurtful blow I would receive was hearing that my father had been murdered. He was forced into a car by two drug addicts and taken down a road not too far from where I went to elementary school. They shot him in the neck and left him to bleed out in a ditch. The murderer's son was in one of my classes, and I had to endure that as well. My bus route went by the murder scene, so I tried not to ride the bus to my grandmother's house as much, and there were issues with the Green Acres bus route.

If I didn't hurry when the bell rang, I would get left at school. My family bought me a car at age 14 with a permit, and they never knew why I was begging for a car. No one ever asked me if I needed professional counseling; not sure why not. My mom was suffering really badly in the first year. She was in a depression and scared to drive in the dark for a long time.

When my mother heard the news, it was as if she broke down again. Even if the two of them were not together, they both deeply loved each other. My dad never remarried after my mom, but my mother remarried years later after his death. He never really talked about the bad parts of the relationship. He would just always encourage me to love my mom and look after my family.

He wanted her back, and perhaps she thought to have him back also, but time wasn't on their side. My dad was a very humble man who loved his family even if it was separated. The funeral was small, and the service was moving. I can remember feeling numb and at a loss for words. It hurt me so badly because it was like his life was snatched away from us in a moment, too soon. When we got to the church, I sat beside my dad's mom on the corner, and I was trying to be strong. I was angry and sad at the same time. My sister had to be carried out.

My mom sat in the crowd, and it was the last funeral she ever went to. When she lost her mom, sister, and grandmother, she did not attend those funerals. Years later, she told me that she couldn't sit up at the front with me because she couldn't see him in the coffin, lifeless.

Now, I understand what she meant, but back then, I didn't understand why she didn't sit up at the front with me.

I recall getting in the funeral car with my sister and aunt. We went to the grave site for the final commencement, and once they lowered him into the ground, we were brought back to the funeral car. I got on my knees to look out the back window as we were driving off. I just didn't want to leave my daddy. I saw the snow falling on top of his grave. Christmas and New Year holidays were hard for me for years because he died right after Christmas and was buried right after the New Year.

My dad was far from perfect, but he was leaving behind two daughters, a wife, and two families that did love him. It was a somber day, and I don't remember much else after I got home from the funeral. I was in bed for two weeks. I just didn't want to live. I was truly fatherless now, unlike before, when I would often have visits from him.

I will now have nothing, no visits, no phone calls, no seeing him when I get off the school bus, nothing. One night during those two weeks, I had a faint dream about my dad, and he told me, in the dream, "Get up and go on with your life. I am okay and you will be too. Go on, and be the best that you can be and do good with your life. Be better than me and your mom."

I never had another dream like that about him before or again. I had simple instructions to push forward with my life, but I still had so many unanswered questions.

Chapter Three

If I had known how to ask the right questions, I could have avoided so much pain as a youth. Do you feel there are questions you don't ask because you are afraid of the answers? Maybe you are skipping out on going to counseling because your family has always thought counseling was just for crazy folks or unnecessary in the black community. Many feel it will work itself out on its own. It won't.

My life didn't begin to turn for the better until I started to be a willing participant in my healing. The unanswered questions I had run from, I carried for years in my heart. When my demand for having all of my questions answered fell off, that was when I knew I needed to accept that I could not change my family dynamic. As I got older, I learned the true meaning of learning to love your mother and father.

Children have a way of judging their parents because they think they have a right. A right to be mad or say what they should have done. The truth is, we don't. Everyone has a right to make their own choices, and we have to love and respect people. Even though my father is not here with me, I still honor him. They didn't have to have me, and they could have thought about their own survival and ended my life, or given me up.

These trials help to make me a better mother who communicates and desires the best for my children. I realized that leaving children with others who are stronger in certain areas could be the best way to show love. My aunt couldn't have children, but she was older, married, and more stable. I resided with my aunt on and off until I permanently stayed with her when I started grade school at age 5.

She never made me feel unwelcome. I know bringing me into her home was a challenge for not only her, but also her husband. They stayed in a two-bedroom house, but the second room was occupied by her stepson and my uncle, whom she also took in as her own. There was no room for me, but she found a way.

I stayed with them and shared their bedroom. I slept in my own bed at the foot of their bed. It was a tight space, but when you love people, you make it work. I thank her husband, my uncle, too, because he never complained and made me feel welcome.

When I was 10 years old, my aunt bought a larger house so I could have my own room. It was one of the nicest and thoughtful things she could have done. She didn't have to increase her bills or change her life so much for me, but she did it for all of us and to make sure we had a better living environment. She was willing to do things my parents could not or did not do for me, and I will forever be grateful.

I learned that the people you should be focusing on are the ones who choose to have something to do with you. Those who choose to participate in your life instead of dwelling on the things you can't change. My uncle didn't replace my father, but he became a necessary father figure I needed in my life. My parents and I were close, but there are people in your life who can grow closer to you than your parents, and that is fine too.

We can resent the people who we think want to take our parents' place, but the truth is that they just want to love you and help you fill a hole that they might have too. I was a child, and although my aunt couldn't have children, she loved helping children. I like to think that I was an answer to my aunt's prayer, like how she was an answer to mine. We both wanted to make God happy with how we treated people. It is not a one-sided thing when God is in it, and he was.

Choosing my aunt Lois and George because I knew that they would have the time to spend with me is surprising. Crazy how a three-year-old could have thought this rationally, being so young. At first, I was thinking, *What? She went up the street back home?* I didn't know the details of the situation at the time. When my mom left my dad, I did feel that she left me, too. It was confusing and heart-jerking to wake up to the commotion, and I struggled with the trauma of abandonment for years into my adulthood, only to learn that I was never abandoned.

Now you are understanding more why I needed counseling. I had to unpack the pain I had that night and the words I had not expressed. When I told my dad I would live with my aunt, his reply was, "Okay, then. I will visit you over there." My mom's response was a lot the same. They visited me often but struggled to have the means to care for me.

To think now as an adult, how a three-year-old could be entrusted to make a life decision shows the responsibility put on children when having young parents. I can remember Lois having to work sometimes two jobs. My aunt worked at a nursing home, Riverside Nursing Home, when I was small. She would take me to see my great-grandmother often for them to keep me while she worked.

My great-grandmother's name was Alice Ruth King. Shirley King was my mother's mom, and they both lived in the house together. Crazy to see four generations coming together in one house regularly, but that was my younger years. Neither of them had a husband, but my grandma Shirley had a boyfriend.

His name was Jimmy Bolden, and he's the father of my last uncle that my grandmother had. I'm not sure why they never married because I would see him so often. My grandmother worked a regular job as a custodian at Newton High and then Eastside High. Before that, she was a cook at East Newton, so she had always been in the school system.

The only other job I can recall her having was Henderson's, which was the restaurant before she got into the school system. But every day, I would get dropped off by Lois at my great-grandmother's, and we would clean the house and do things together. Everybody would go to work, and it would be just us hanging out. She showed me how to make up beds, sweep the floor, and keep a clean house. I can recall being about maybe four or five years old, making beds and tucking the pillows like a hotel maid.

When I say sweep, I mean we had to make our

own broom and sweep the yard! We swept the yards then because the yards didn't have any grass. We had to sweep with something called a brush broom, and how we made it was by collecting sticks from the briar patches. We tied them together with a scarf or an old shirt. Nothing went to waste, not food, not fabric, not space; not nothing.

My great-grandmother also taught me how to mop, probably when I was maybe a little older than six or seven. When I started going to school, I got dropped off by the bus there with her. Many afternoons, I remembered mopping floors when I got home. What I loved was that she taught me to do after mopping was cooking. I never actually cooked, though; I just enjoyed watching her do it.

I wasn't the only one gifted to spend time with Alice; other kids sometimes were in the house as well as I got older. My cousins, Valencia, Delisha, Samuel, and Robin, would sometimes spend time there too. We all loved Grandma Alice. Robin was older than we were. There was only a few years difference amongst the rest of us, but I was the first great-grandchild.

When I got to be about six or seven, that's when Valencia, Sam, and Delisha came into the household. These are my aunt Lisa's children, which was my mom's sister on her mom's side, and they all lived there. With my grandma's help, I would sometimes babysit Sam, Valencia, and Delisha when Lisa was out.

Lisa was very crafty, and she used her talent all the time. She made clothes and always did my mom's hair. My mom often contributed to the household by doing everyone's hair growing up, too.

Another auntie in the same house was my aunt

Crystal. She wasn't really my aunt, but she was my mom's first cousin, whom my grandmother raised us to call auntie. She was the one who took me to see my first movie in theaters!

I remember when she took me and my uncle, Kenny, to see our first movie at the Newton Plaza. The first movie I ever saw was "The Gremlins." I was so excited to go to the movies for the first time at six or seven.

Each woman and child in that house gave me something I needed. As I grew older, I took the good stuff and a little piece of my morals from each person. So from three to nine, my childhood was very good, at least I thought it was. In the small town of Jamestown in Covington, Georgia, we had a lot of elders.

This community was tight, the kind that if someone saw you being bad, your grandma would know within the hour. They would visit each other and stay awhile to keep each other company. We had a neighbor, her name was Hazel Binder, and she was a retired school teacher. I can remember her coming to cook and bake with my great-grandmother, Alice. She taught me my ABCs using access baking flour as we waited for things to bake.

Another elder was Mamie Kelly. We called her Miss Sweet Pea. I can remember my great-grandmother and I going fishing with her, and she brought her granddaughter, Terricas Critton. We would play on the lake while our grandmothers fished. On these trips, I remember learning my timetables from Terricas. She taught me my timetables long before I was supposed to know them.

Then I can remember staying in Cathleen Wil-

Chapter Three

liams' house on Third Street. In that house, we had some very good times. My best friend and childhood friend, Marcie Williams, lived across the street. I have a cousin we call Mon. We would play in the streets at night, and ride bicycles back and forth between the streets. It was pretty safe because everybody knew everybody in the neighborhood, and you could pretty much play in the dark on the different streets because people would look out for you.

The elders were a piece of my life that I loved. Our house might have looked raggedy, but I remember us being so happy. I can remember the roof leaks, freezing toilets like at Lois's house, being common problems we learned to live through. Some might have called us poor, but we had rich memories. I can remember growing up with my cousin, Demetrius, and my uncles, Anthony and David, who are more like brothers to me. I was always around them when I lived with Lois and George.

It was Anthony, Lois, George, Demetrius, David, and myself who lived in that two-bedroom house. The bathroom wasn't big at all. In the kitchen, you can heat the whole house with that single stove. That's how small it was. Now you understand why I had to sleep on a daybed at the bottom of Lois and George's bed.

The house used to leak, and it used to be so cold in the winter that the toilet would freeze over. Can you imagine that Georgia used to be that cold? We had to put a heater in the bathroom to heat the bathroom just so we could take a shower. Entering the bathroom with a coat on was normal because it was just so cold in there. We only had one space heater for heating, and the bathroom took that. In the living room, we had a floor model TV, and our dining room was inside the living room. The living room had a gas heater.

Like I told you, it was small, but what was really weird was that we had the biggest front porch that I had ever seen. I loved it. I used to play on it and the sidewalk leading off the steps. Marcie, Mon, and I used to play hopscotch on the sidewalk and rest on the steps. Again, I didn't have my own room, and I can remember experiencing my first tragedy. Lois had a cousin whom we called Cookie. He was supposed to be raised with me, and when he lived with us, he stayed on the couch.

I remember him sleeping on one end and me on the other when I was young. (I didn't get a day bed by Lois' bed until I got bigger.) One day, I remember his uncle, Bubba, coming to take him back to Atlanta. He was kicking him and screaming as he left. Lois didn't have legal custody of him, so she could not do anything to stop it. He had stayed with us for a few years.

A couple of years after he left, he was murdered at Perry Holmes in Atlanta. We got the news by seeing his face on the front page of a news article. This was the first real tragedy I had ever experienced because Cookie and I were like brother and sister.

There were certainly challenges with trying to raise all of us. One of the biggest challenges was scheduling. My aunt, for one, didn't have a regular work schedule. Her schedule changed week to week, so finding a second job was also difficult because the first had open availability.

Their finances were off because how can you plan to do more when you don't know what you have? They were not highly educated, but they knew how to survive.

Chapter Three

They knew the basic life necessities, but luxuries they did not have.

After working an 8-hour shift, my aunt would come home and have to go to the laundry mat to wash our clothes. We didn't have a washer and dryer in our home while living in Jamestown. There was nowhere to put it if we could afford a set. Going to the laundry mat was a task by itself. She had to wash and fold the clothes there, then travel fifteen or sixteen miles down the road, where we would put the clothes away. After all of that, she had to cook, and I am sure she went to bed exhausted on many nights.

Everybody's bedtime seemed to be picked based on her work schedule, too. We had to go to bed so she could get up to go to work the next day. We tried to take off some of the pressure on her life by keeping the house clean. I heard a few arguments about money between my aunt and uncle, and it made me want to do something as I got older to help.

The way we were living was something else. I remember one of my cousins spending the night, and we told him not to sleep in the recliner. He was so tired that when he came in, that's where he fell asleep. The problem, the roof leaked where he was sleeping. He almost got frostbite on his feet from the water dripping down on them. He didn't even feel it. We had to heat his feet up to keep him from having hot frostbite from the leaky roof.

The roof wasn't the only problem. Going out back was a death trap, too. You would open the back door, thinking to step your foot on the deck, only your foot would go through the boards because the wood had rotted out and needed to be replaced. But where was that money going to come from?

None of the stuff that needed to be replaced ever was. Eventually, that place was torn down, and there is a mobile home that sits there now. Sometimes I can close my eyes and I can picture what it used to be like in Jamestown, because even though we weren't in the best living conditions, it housed some of the happiest moments in my life, because I had my great-grandmother. I had my dad, and some of the people in the community that I love, like Ms. Binder, Mr. Binder, Ms. Avery, Mr. and Mrs. Freeman, and Mr. Kelly. These were all good people.

They always looked out for me. There was a pathway from our house leading to my great-grandmother's house. And I can recall Ms. Avery, who wouldn't let anybody go through that pathway, allowing me to shortcut through there to get to my grandmother's house. She would watch me cross through her yard and walk into my grandmother's house.

She wouldn't let her dog bother me either, who guarded her yard. Sometimes when she was at work, Ms. Binder would tell me, "Well, you come cut across my yard and go up there." It was nice to feel special. I can remember going to my dad's mom's house. My great-grandmother, Maddie Stinson, who was my dad's grandmother, would sometimes walk and meet my mama's great-grandmother, Alice. I remember hanging out with Nikki, my cousins, and Candace from my dad's side.

We would play at my grandmother's house, and that's the only people that I was kind of around that were in my age bracket, because on my mom's side, there was kind of a gap in the grandkids. But I used to love to go with them. We would play in the dirt together because we had no grass and weren't allowed to play in the house; we had so much fun together.

Even though her name is Maddie Stinson, we called her Mama Matt. She would sneak us little snacks and stuff. And it was just good to be around a group of cousins who were girls. And then I had two male cousins, whom I was around a lot, Emilo and Fred.

I remember one time, my aunt Patricia, whom we called Pat, was taking her kids to the Bobby Brown concert. I wanted to go so badly, but I didn't get a chance to go because I was too little. There were many other events she brought us to throughout the years. I also remember my uncle, Charlie Ruth, who, when I was about nine years old, took me to Atlanta to go to Six Flags.

It was my first time ever going to Six Flags. I remember my first time ever seeing Atlanta. I went with my grandmother, Pauline, and her boyfriend at the time, Mr. Bill, and my cousin Nikki. The four of us were going to see my grandmother's aunt.

Seeing Six Flags as we drove through the city, I remember thinking, *I wanna go there one day*. I can remember all the tall buildings and how long the drive was. My grandmother, Pauline, was excited to show me the city and introduce me to family. There are a lot of memories in my head from my small neighborhood. I can't tell you every person or event, but most of my memories growing up were more good than bad.

I didn't have any real expectations when it came to living with Lois because I had been accustomed to how she was as a person. I knew there were certain things that I could not do. Sometimes I didn't like the fact that

I wasn't living with both of my parents. Other than that, there wasn't really anything I didn't like besides not having my own room, which changed as I got older.

Even though my life had some stuff in it that would make me think I was less fortunate growing up, it made me more grateful than bitter. I didn't complain, and every little ray of sunshine in my life reminded me of the hearts people had for me. I was grateful for my great-grandparents on both my mom's and my dad's sides.

I remember my dad taking me to see his dad sometimes and his dad's mom. My dad's grandmother's name was Lillian. I only saw her once in my life, but I remember that she was a very pretty lady. I also remember meeting Alice's daddy before.

I have a memory like an elephant, and I am glad to have hung out around the seniors in my community. I didn't know the full benefit then, but to know what I do now, I was blessed beyond measure. I remember being with Alice, and her father came into the house drunk; she nurtured him sober with gentleness. He knocked over some of her dishes, and she told me, "This is my daddy. His name is Eddie Lee White, and this is my brother. His name is Dempsey. And I remember Uncle Dempsey having a patch and me asking my grandmother, "What is that patch on his eye for?"

She said, "His eye got put out. He only got one eye, but that's my brother." I recall seeing a lot of stuff. I recall that people were happy back then. They planted gardens as a regular daily function.

My grandmother, Shirley, had a garden in her backyard. Sometimes I would go out there with her and help her pick the cucumbers and the collard greens or whatever she had planted. I remember Miss Sweet Pea having a garden also, and this is why you couldn't just go walking through people's yards.

There are a lot of good memories from my childhood from ages three to nine. A good memory that happened at ten, a wow moment I had prayed for, though I don't remember really expecting to get it, was my own room. With my large family, everyone shared a room, a couch, or some kind of space.

I guess that's another way I knew I was special, too.

Chapter Four

Getting to have my own room was a process, and I am grateful for it. I saw what it was like living in that two-bedroom house with problems everywhere. Wearing coats to go to the bathroom, having a leaky roof, and a toilet that froze over were something we all hoped to get past.

I remember asking my aunt to get a job that would allow her to get the weekends off so she could spend more time with me. I loved my aunt and everybody, but I didn't spend as much time with her as I had wanted. She was willing to work and sacrifice for all of us, and I just wanted her to be able to enjoy the fruits of her labor, you know.

When I lived with her, though we had no extra money I knew of, I can't remember ever going hungry or not having what I needed for school and things. She always made sure I had what I needed, and I didn't think we struggled financially. My aunt worked hard, and she would tell me that she was working on changing her job. She didn't make my request of working less happen right away, but she would find a way.

Sometimes we can feel that no one is hearing us because what we ask for we don't see yet. She told me she was working on it, and I had to be settled in my own heart to trust her word. She was a commendable woman whom I don't remember lying. It was easy to trust her and be patient, because I saw what she did each day for me and my cousins.

Before I turned 11, she moved into a house in Greenacres, which was a neighborhood in Covington, Georgia. We moved to 6258 Greenacre Drive, and I'll never forget it because it was the very first time that I ever had my own room. I was so shocked.

My uncle and my cousin, who were considered my brothers, Demetrius and Anthony, were happy for me. And my other cousin, who was also like an uncle to me, was happy too. His name was David, and the three boys shared a room together. They had two bunk beds and a twin bed in their room. I had my own room, and my aunt Lois and George had a room. I got my own room, I think, because there were no other girls.

Moving into a three-bedroom house, with one working bathroom, was a dream come true. We had to share a bathroom, sure, but at least we didn't have to wear coats in the house. The floorboards all worked. No more leaky roof! We moved up when we got to live in that house.

And I can remember going through middle school there, and my aunt finally getting a job at Palmer Stone Elementary, in the kitchen as a cook during those years. She was able to have the weekends off, only to work during the school day. Her change in schedule meant I could have more time with her, and we could do things together. It was a prayer prayed and answered. I was so glad when she changed jobs.

The next four years were uneventful in the sense that everything was normal. I still saw family. I lived with no issues in school, and my parents were still living and doing great. Now, in 1994, after I turned 14 years old, that's when trauma would hit again when my dad was murdered in December of 1994.

This shot up my world and changed my life in a lot of different ways. When my dad was murdered in a case of mistaken identity, I kind of knew before anybody ever told me because I felt it, believe it or not. When you have a strong bond with your parent or your children, you can feel or sense when something's wrong. I did sense something was wrong with him, but I wasn't sure of what.

My dad passed away from a gunshot wound to the neck. He was in a car with two men that he knew dumped him out of the car into a ditch on a rural road, and he bled out. I remember the shockwave in the family going to his funeral. It was hard to be there and see him like I did. As I write this, I remember one time being with my dad when he worked on cars.

I was young, but my dad made me comfortable around cars, engines, and anything in his workspace. He used to test engines and do repairs on cars. I used to see him wipe what I thought was super glue on parts. When I got older, I had a spark plug that was having an issue, and I wiped super glue around the connection instead of sealant. I learned that lesson as an adult, and trying to fix my car in a pinch. My solution was temporary, of course, but it was a moment in my life where my dad came through.

The funeral was at a time when we all should have been happy to welcome in the next year with joy. It was the day after New Year's when we buried him. I guess they tried to push it to after the holidays, but the change in life made New Year's that year somber anyhow.

My dad was supposed to teach me to drive the next year because I would have been getting my learner's permit for my license. It wasn't just about driving; I grieved my dad's death, I felt I was robbed, and I wouldn't have a normal family life ever. I didn't have the perfect story, but I had hopes that it would get better.

My uncle George was kind, and he always helped me to have a father figure, even before my dad died. He didn't have to treat me like his daughter, but he did. I remember him giving me hugs and speaking words of encouragement about my life. When I was 14 years old and wanted to get a car, I went to my uncle to help me get it done. He was like that with anything; if you needed help, he was a solid person to lean on.

I didn't know how to process my father's death, so I did the only thing I could do: bury myself in the things I could control, like work and school. My uncle helped me to get there and was very supportive and pushed me to excel. I buried my thoughts about thinking of the future by allowing people who loved me to take my mind off losing my dad. I was hiding in plain sight with my job. What I did to self-medicate my own internal war, my mom and grandparents, aunts and uncles, had no idea of how to stop–I didn't know how to make it stop. They only saw the positive results and assumed I was well, though I was struggling.

Chapter Four

At the funeral, I wasn't sure how to respond openly with everyone watching. I couldn't really cry because in my head, I felt I had to be strong. I had a sister who was just a couple of months younger than me. At that funeral, although my parents would fight off and on through the years, they had tender moments that hinted at them possibly getting back together again. I saw the death of that on my mother's face as she continued to have a blank stare for months. Everybody around me was crying and grieving, and I was standing, seemingly unmoved. Crazy how I could have this super large family, and how I could feel so alone in those moments. I was grieving in my own way. It took me some time to go back into my ninth-grade class after it all.

Seeing the dirt piled on top one shovel at a time was cemented in my mind, and it would replay over and over again, so his death stayed fresh in my heart for years. I sat on my bed and I thought about nothing. I could only feel pain as I lay back on my bed. For days after the funeral, I didn't know how I was going to live without my dad. Around this time, I had met the new guy my mom was dating, who became the father to my younger sister, Shanice. They had been dating for about two years. The two of them met when I was 12 years old, so my sister Shanice was 2 when my dad died.

I always wanted another sibling because I was my mother's only child. My dad had another daughter who's just a few months younger than me. And she had two other siblings. I felt alone, and now I wouldn't have to be on my mom's side. The only thing I disliked was that my momma waited until I was 12 years old to have another child.

But the inconvenience of our ages became a

non-issue with all the fun I had with my baby sister, Shanice. Even though she wasn't my dad's child, my dad did treat Shanice like she was. When she was a newborn, she was a pretty baby, and I felt like she was a real-life baby doll; she was so well-mannered and cute.

Shanice's dad was there for the first part of her life. About a year and a half, it could be a little longer. He tried to be a father to me until I was about 15 years old. Then he became an absent father to both of us. It was hurtful because it wasn't like we could go to my father to fill his shoes; we just missed out. We faced a lot of stuff together growing up, even though we didn't live together; my goal was still for us to be close.

Sometimes I wish she could have moved in with me so I could spend more time with her. She lived with my grandmother, Shirley, and our mom. After all these years, my Grandmother Shirley still took the bulk of responsibility for Shanice, like how she and my aunt Lois took care of me. I used to have mixed emotions about that because I'm like, why does she have to do so much? What made my mom keep my little sister and send me away? I guess I got a little jealous, but not to wish ill-will, I just wanted to be with her, but I wasn't.

My grandmother was a little bit more settled when Shanice came. As I got older in life and I had all my own kids, I began to understand why it was the way it was for us growing up. My Aunt Lois did ask for Shanice a couple of times, but I think my mama said no because she missed out on raising me.

It was nice that she and my mom grew to be close, and she had an experience that I didn't. I wasn't mad about that because Aunt Lois was great, but I would have liked to be more involved in her life when I was younger, like Shanice. The two of them were able to bond in a way that I was not, I feel. But I am glad that I am close to my sister, and she looks up to me.

I'm her big sister, but I think Shanice sees me more like a mother figure, because I was always there to pick her up when she fell. I'm still trying not to be so involved in her life that I handicap her in her adult life. I don't wanna cripple her from being responsible. And that's one of the challenges that I'm trying to overcome.

I went to Eastside High School when I returned to school. It was a transition school, so nobody was there before us, and there were no upperclass students. I liked being part of the oldest group at school.

We were the first graduating class out of Eastside High in Covington, Georgia. Every year that we advanced, they added the next grade level until we would graduate. When we graduated, it became a full-blown high school. In middle school, I went to Sharp Middle School.

It was an old school with lead-painted walls; it was so old. We could have all been sick from attending that school. I went there all three years of middle school, and some time after we left, they condemned and closed the school. It really should have been a lawsuit for how we were treated and made to learn in an environment they knew was dangerous for us all.

The building has since been torn down. That school probably needed more renovations than the cost to just rebuild. I can remember being dropped off early before Lois had to go to work. I would sit in the cafeteria, and Mr. Crutchfield, the custodian, would let me in. He would make sure I was okay and nobody bothered me.

I would eat breakfast and go on to class. I can remember getting confused as to which bus to get on because Lois was in between working at the nursing facility and working at the school. Sometimes she would tell me to take the bus home to my grandmother's house in Jamestown. I would have to run from class to catch the bus to Green Acres, and I didn't know about 70% of the people.

One time, I got off the bus, and no one was waiting for me. I went to my grandma's house, and no one was there either. I wasn't worried at first, but it wasn't until I heard something fall in the kitchen that I got freaked out.

I ran out of the house so fast and went down to the neighbor's house on Third Street. I stayed there until my grandmother got back. The only reason why I was there by myself was because my aunt had to take my grandma to the doctor. It was this event that pushed me to get my own car so I could drive home and be around people. I didn't like being home alone or not having adequate transportation to and from school.

Going back to school after my dad's passing, I remember praying no one would ask me questions, although I needed them to do something. I had a couple of cousins who checked on me, but it was very difficult to hear the questions, "Are you alright?" or the statement, "I heard about your dad. I'm praying for you." I know they wanted to help, but I am not sure how it impacted me at the time. I was fighting with my new reality, and the comments and questions reminded me of that.

Chapter Four

Yes, death was part of life. I went to a lot of funerals for family members who grew old or got sick and died. I've experienced death. I lost grandparents and things of that nature, but they were ill, and that made sense to me. This was so sudden and out of the blue, so I struggled with accepting it. The more I tried to forget, the more it circled back in front of my face.

Murder to me is a different kind of thing because it is so unexpected. It gives you no warning, so you can prepare yourself; it just yanks you down by the pressure of the word death. I could hardly catch my breath, like being on some rides at Six Flags.

Going to work after school wasn't a chore, and it was something I enjoyed. I saw how having a job could help me excel and get the things I wanted. I wanted a car, and the job was how I would afford it. I knew I had to keep up with my grades to keep working, so I took school way more seriously.

When I could afford the car, I wondered who would take me to get it. I also needed to get a license. How would I get that? I feared no one, but my uncle David & George helped me get my driver's license. It was David who helped me to learn how to drive.

Later, when it was time for me to get a car, George called a friend who was able to sell me a car for $500. It wasn't a race car and couldn't drive over 60 mph, but it was what I needed at the time. It was a used car and would likely last me a year before it died, but it was okay. I would be driving it until then. Getting this car added more responsibilities to my plate.

It was a task trying to get and keep the car. I was

getting Social Security from my dad, and I remember working two jobs at one time while being in high school to ride around in a car. I got a work permit and got my first job at McDonald's. I didn't stay there long before I went to another popular food chain, Taco Bell. Not long after working there, I left to work for the Newton County Board of Education, where I started to order supplies, and that developed my skills with numbers.

In school, I had a very good math teacher, Julia Boyum, who helped me through a lot of it. I buried myself into learning numbers because it didn't deal with emotions or topics I was burying. It was simple, and the answers were finite. I didn't feel I was getting the proper help that I needed to be successful as an adult overcoming adolescence. I had work ethic from my aunt and family, but I wasn't taught how to manage my emotions. I tried to mature in this way, but my heart was all over the place.

I tried to date when I got 16, but it was a failed attempt to find my father in them. I didn't realize it at the time, but I wanted to see him again somewhere or anywhere. I was desperate to find my father again, and I did make some poor decisions because of it, but also good ones.

Between 15 and 16 years old, I knew I wanted a better car, and I would need some help to do it. By the time I was 16, my mom did very little to help me support myself because I could provide for myself with my job and my dad's social security. I was glad I didn't need her too much because she took my dad's death worse than I did. They were good friends even though they both chose to move on. I wanted my mom to focus on taking care of my sister, too.

Chapter Four

My mom developed a strong phobia of driving at night since the day my dad died. No matter what was going on during the day, she would insist on getting home before dark. It was kind of depressing for my mom because she lived with my grandmother still. I will be down there visiting or doing something for my grandmother.

My mom would be near panic to get in before dark. It took a toll on her and her relationship as well. My sister's dad tried to intervene before my dad died, as far as coming to see me get awards in the eighth grade and everything. My parents weren't very active in my school life because they were always working, so seeing him show up was very kind of him.

I didn't see it then, but that was his doing and not my mother's. When he left, I really didn't have any active parent or step-parent in my life. The only advantage I had was when I was in high school, age 14, 15, 16, my grandmother was the custodian there. She would peek in on me to see if I was alright and what I was doing. My mother later dated Bud, and he was there for me and my sister until they broke up when my sister became a teenager.

My aunt Lois and George kept a roof over my head, and they did what they could. They had their financial situation going on, and money wasn't the best. They had three boys to raise, and I knew keeping us all wasn't cheap. They did what they could for me, and I was grateful. I can remember when I got my car from the dealer; my mom cosigned for me. I was grateful she did that for me, and I was committed to keeping up with the payments. It was kind of a sweet 16 gift, and my uncle George told me, "Your daddy told me to take care of you, and I'm gonna do that." I remember him getting my windows tinted on my car for Christmas.

I can remember the repo coming to get my car, too. Nobody would help me with payments or figuring out what I needed. They signed, but I felt like I was on my own with this car. In that moment, I needed active parents and not just caring family members. I didn't have that. I had to choose between paying for my car and going to prom. The sad part is that I couldn't do either because I had an uncle who lived in the house who went to jail.

He had racked up $1,500 in "Collect calls" on my phone, and I had to decide between paying that bill or paying for my car. But that wasn't a choice. I was young, so the car wasn't in my name, nor was the phone bill; the phone was in my aunt's name, and my car was in my mother's name. I had to pay that phone bill because of that, and I was hoping to scrape by to pay the car. Only I got into a car wreck, and I had to pay for that too, because I was at fault.

It was a hard pill to swallow. I lost all the money I had worked for and the car that was the prize. Even worse, I left my mom in debt, and it burned in my stomach to know that I could be the reason she now couldn't get anything else. I sat there on the floor thinking of what I could do to change things.

I was never the type to make a mess and leave it for someone else to clean up. I felt like if I ditched it, I would help catch the fallout and work to fix it. That's when I learned you could write things off as a loss through filing for bankruptcy.

To save my mother's credit and many other family members, I learned how to file for bankruptcy. When I got that car off her report, everyone else wanted me to do theirs. I worked on bankruptcies for ten family members

Chapter Four

who got cleared ,also. It was nice to be part of the solution for how they got their lives on track, another thing that God gave me to show that I was special, math, and business.

So that one experience led me to heal the whole family, and it was very painful. And I can remember going to my aunt and her saying, "It's going to be okay. I'm gonna sign and get you another car," and she did. From that moment on, my grandmother, my aunt, and my uncle kept me in a car.

I remember my aunt Lisa signing for me to get a car one time, and she was about to buy a house. My family came through for me, I could see it then, but that day the repo man came, I felt alone, although I wasn't. Sometimes it has to rain, bad things or things we don't like happen, so we can discover something new about ourselves. We shine the brightest when it is dark outside.

My aunt needed to get out of the car payment, and I remember trading out the car just so she could have her credit back to get her house.

Chapter Five

Have you ever done something that you thought at the time made sense, but when the years carried on, you realized you made the worst decision you could have made? There are choices we can make in our lives that we can quickly regret, and a choice I made concerning my education was a mistake littered with guilt and shame. I was smart in school, but I had a problem.

In high school, I was dealing with a lot. I thought everything was too much, and I felt like a heavy weight was on my shoulders that I couldn't bear at the time. I was burnt out on life, classes, and doing stuff that didn't seem to improve my life. School felt like a place adults send their children to for babysitting.

I wanted to live my life. I wanted something for my life, and I did understand how school could be a big enough part of that. It was my hunger to change my immediate circumstances that led me to push to finish school early. This is one of the hardest stories I've ever had to tell because there was nothing else for me to do in school. So I got out.

I finished school early, and after my first semester of 12th grade, I had all the credits and had taken the classes I needed to graduate. So I went back to March with my graduating class in May of '98. Here's the problem: I am a great student but a terrible test taker. I had difficulty passing social studies and the science test required for me to graduate. I needed something to become bigger and more important to me than fear. By the time we got ready to walk, I had passed the social studies test.

A lot of people don't know this, but I didn't pass the science exam, and I was embarrassed. It's hard to think of how one test could rob you of all the rest of the work you have completed, but in my case, it did temporarily. This is the reason I didn't apply for college. I went back later to take the test, and the result was the same. I quit trying, and I went and got a job. I needed to start working to pay off my car and still live life. I refused to be a failure in my own eyes because of a test.

I landed a permanent job at a place called Universal Solution, which specialized in the pharmaceutical industry. While I worked there, they changed their name, not sure why, but I guess it was for rebranding. I was there for five years, and yes, I started while in high school and stayed through my early 20s. When I turned twenty, I tried to go to the Army as they were going to help me pass my science exit exam.

I was excited that I would get a break from working hard and be able to work smarter by getting an education. My grandparents always emphasized that. The big problem, days away from enlisting, I get the confirmation that I was pregnant. I had my first kid at 21 and my second kid at 22. My financial picture was growing difficult,

Chapter Five

and having two young babies about a year apart didn't make life easier.

I remember thinking of other things I could do to help myself. I knew working the job I had was limited, so I sought ways to increase my money and better the life circumstances for me and my children. I remember I applied for a job in the office, and I'll never forget the reaction and response the HR lady gave me. When I went in there ready to speak about advancement, she looked me in my eyes and told me matter-of-factly, "You will never be successful in an office position because you are too country."

I felt crushed, judged, misunderstood, and mad. My anger quickly transitioned to pain, and I started to believe the limiting statement this lady, who didn't know me, had said about my life. I was heading into a downward spiral mentally and did not know how to get out. I can remember leaving her office, actually thinking maybe she was right, and that is why I failed science.

I thought that I needed to go back to school to prove the lady wrong. Maybe to convince myself, too, that I was smart and good enough to do whatever I wanted to do with my life. I thought getting my GED would prove that.

But school was still on the back burner because life was coming at me fast. In addition to having a baby at 21, I got married before baby number one came. Our marriage wasn't stable for too long. I was battling my own emotional problems, and he was having a hard time being faithful.

On top of our social and emotional challenges,

we had financial hardship too. It was hard to find me in the midst of all this. We were filing for divorce because I found out about his infidelity, and I could not bear it with everything else I had to manage.

He had another child, and the birth dates between our children are only months apart. My son was born in August, and I believe her child was born in January. I couldn't handle the drama, and I felt I shouldn't have to, so I decided to get a divorce. I can remember during the most difficult time of my life being laid off from the job I couldn't afford to feed three people on a hundred and eighteen dollars a week unemployment.

I can remember going back home to my aunt's house, and I went to DFCS shortly after that. The DFCS lady, Sonya, looked me in the face and saw my potential before I opened my mouth. I needed direction and a plan. She asked me, "What do you wanna do?"

She continued, "Do you want some food stamps? You want a check? Housing assistance, what?"

Confidently, I replied, "No. I just want daycare assistance for my children. I wanna work." The lady didn't say anything, she just looked at me and nodded her head. She typed something on the computer, and she sent me to Brenda Tanner at the Georgia unemployment office.

Brenda was helpful in helping me rewrite my resume and land a job. The job was supposed to be temporary, but I was there for eleven years. I was the only lady on and off for eleven years in that office. I learned a lot. I confided in my boss about my high school diploma one day, and I remember what he said.

He said, "Go back and get it." He had a fatherly tone that I needed to hear to encourage me. I decided I would go back after a few years on this job. When I went to get a GED, instead of feeling great or empowered, I just kept coming back to how stupid it was. I don't know what I was thinking about getting a GED when I was smart enough to pass the science class.

It seemed like I was running, but I knew I shouldn't and that I couldn't. I needed to face this class and whatever it represented in my life. I went to the GED classes, and I tried to see this GED course as part of my story, but I didn't. Something just kept saying, "No, this is not you. You only need to pass that science class, so go do it."

Eventually, I stopped taking the GED class because I started to rekindle my belief in myself. I knew I was smart enough to pass it. It was after I had my two kids and was on my own that I decided to burn hours at the library studying. I applied myself and went back after 5 years.

When I went back to take just the science part of the high school graduation test, I passed! Not only did I do that, but after I graduated, I went and got an apartment by myself with my two kids. Passing this test unlocked blessings for me and proved something about me.

I was strong, resilient, and capable of anything I put my mind to. No matter how long it took me, I knew I could do great things with God pushing me and sending the right people to come in and help me. I was able to pay all of my bills, and a year after that, I bought a house on my own.

I was happy with how much I had accomplished so far. I was taking care of my children, owned a home, but the bills did trickle up. I realized the education I had, although I was proud, wasn't enough to outpace my bills. I needed more, I needed more education.

I remember going into the HR office and asking what other positions I could try out for. They told me that many of the jobs I had my eyes on required a college degree or more education. I knew going to school would require a sacrifice on my end. I had to balance school, work, and taking care of my children with the help of my aunt and uncle.

I became more resourceful with my time and completed an eight-hour shift in four to five hours. I was committed to being the best I could be, so I started learning everything about the office. When others were out golfing on their breaks, I was running the office by myself. I could have easily felt this was unfair and slowed down, but I didn't let it bother me. I knew what I was building to achieve.

I found out just how smart I was in school. I didn't stop at an associate's degree nor a bachelor's. I went on until I completed my master's program! I learned to love education because I liked the benefits of education. I saw what my grandparents wanted me to see, and I wanted to be that for my two sons. Sometimes I only slept three or four hours a night during my tremendous push and pursuit of education.

It was rough for me, but I never complained. It was the same angel who looked out for me as a child who would offer to help me with my sons, my aunt. She was like, "Let me help you with your kids. I raised you, and I can help with the boys. You're not getting any sleep, and you're trying to get the degree and everything."

Out of love, she also said, "I know you got a lot to do with your finances and everything. Please allow me to help you. It is hard doing all of this by yourself with not a whole lot of help." So that's what I did. I went on and got the degree so that I could financially support myself and my kids when I was between the ages of 27 and 30.

At 27, I also reached another milestone. I bought my first house by myself at age 27, and I didn't have to have nobody to co-sign. I was full of joy, and I can remember it was after my divorce and filing for bankruptcy. I worked to repair my credit so I could buy a house. I couldn't rely on my ex-husband to help me; it was all on me.

I think it was four years after my divorce, and a few years after the credit repair was completed, that I bought my own house. My kids were so happy when we came home to this house. It was a brand new build from the ground, and I remember the builder found out I was a single parent. After hearing that, they gave me a free refrigerator and stove, and gave me my $500 earnest money back.

I was grateful to get the appliances and the $500. I bought the couch we needed for the living room with the money. For the bedrooms, I had enough rooms to give them their own rooms, but they didn't want to be separated. So, I set up an office in the second room.

The boy's room was decorated with matching bedding, and they had their own bathroom. My room was a good size, even with furniture. I loved having my own bathroom that I decorated to my taste. This three-bedroom, two bathroom home made us very happy.

I came to realize we both were just young, and maybe too young to understand the weight of marriage. Neither one of us had been married or seen one as far as I know, that was really successful in our home life. Neither of us went through any real trials to know what marriage would cost us.

I knew that I was trying to have a family, and I guess he was too. Neither one of us had really matured before we were thrown into being parents and then husband and wife. Yes, he cheated, and that was wrong, but I wasn't mature enough to endure what he did to stay with him, either.

I don't feel that I was wrong, but I did mourn a family structure I had planned in my heart that was gone. I wanted to be a wife, married, and take care of my sons with help. This was not the way things should have been, you know? But no one should stay in a situation where love and respect isn't genuine towards each other.

I was struggling to accept the condition in which I found myself. I was debating on if there was something I could have done differently. Was he happier without us, and I was the only one fighting to stay afloat? I was determined not to go anywhere we went together in hopes of not seeing him happy or moving on. I didn't wish him any ill will, I just didn't want to see him.

I don't know why I was so insistent on not going outside when he wasn't raised in my city. I brought him to my town where I grew up and introduced him to my friends from high school and growing up. I wanted to invite him to my world because he grew up more sheltered than me. He didn't experience the dynamics of high school that I knew with clubs and things.

When I introduced him to my city and group of friends, that was when he cheated. He slept with someone I knew from high school, and it felt like a tender betrayal. I don't know if the woman was someone I hadn't known, if that would have made a difference in how I felt. I think it would have stopped me from being uncomfortable in my own city, though.

Those years were hard on me, and I did a lot of thinking. I didn't realize how the absence of my father really took a toll on my life. I wanted a husband, but I also needed a father to help father my children. In this situation, normally, a daughter would lean on her father, but mine was gone. I had been looking for him in the men I dated, and even now.

It took me until I turned twenty-five before I sought help. I knew for this new chapter of my life, I didn't want to carry my pain or shenanigans from my past. I needed to grow and mature, and I believed counseling was a link to having that happen.

I know it is hard to see how divorce could be the right step forward with our beliefs, convictions, and how divorce can tear apart our dreams for a future. But divorcing, I realized real quick, was the best thing to save my future. I was picking wrong, and I needed to reset my life. I realized the bad things that happen in our lives work to our good, too.

I was in an ugly cycle that I needed to escape, and

in some ways, my ex-husband was too. We both needed to grow and learn different things to become better versions of ourselves. So divorce for us was not a bad thing. And if you need to hear this, "Divorce is not a bad thing. I can tell you that because I've been through it."

I did need to be encouraged through the process because it does hurt. I know the situation can also be trying when you have children and are working to see a way forward for everyone. You think about the dangers of marrying someone else in the future, and if you will be too much. The concerns you had without children change when you do. I remember the advice of my grandmother. She used to tell me all the time, "You know, you need to be careful who you bring into your life. You have kids now."

I didn't know the challenges of a blended family. I wasn't sure what my future would look like moving forward, but I thought about it between 17 and 25. When my life changed, I didn't see a relationship ahead of me at that time, because I was too focused on surviving and paying bills. What I was going to feed my children weighed heavier on my heart than dating.

When I wanted to quit because I felt overwhelmed by the challenges of life, I looked to my kids. My children kept me focused and determined to win as I battled my internal and external problems. I knew that my children needed me. Although I faced uncertainty with employment, money, and how to move forward, I drew strength from them.

I stepped out on faith and took a temporary job that led to an eleven-year career. If I didn't start at this job, who's to say if I would have went back to school, finished, and gotten college degrees? I wanted to be in an office, and by God's grace, I got there. I knew opportunities were few because of my lack of education at the time, but God showed me mercy and grace.

I showed my gratitude by working really hard. Getting the job and advancing was not just about the work, but also the social issues that ensued, too. There were those who looked down on me for having two children and didn't know my circumstances. Those I knew who had judged me and determined I would fail. These people didn't want to help me or give me information that they felt would lead me to surpass them.

Inner office dynamics was a different level of street talk I had to learn. I was never a ghetto person, some claimed country, but I didn't know anything about how mean some people could be in this sense. I have always been a hard worker, and I thought that that would be enough to open doors. It did, but it also brought negative attention.

A lot of my coworkers were white men, and that didn't bother me. However, me being black did cause some eyebrows to raise. I heard remarks and slick comments that I learned to look past. I remember wanting to help a co-worker get their check. They lived in a trailer park, and I was told not to take the check to them because I might not make it out.

I was never scared to do my job. I don't know why I was so bold, but I was. I went there and brought him his check, and I remember him telling others, "Hey, this is my HR lady. Don't mess with her. She pays me and makes sure I eat. She's a good person. " Working in HR, you can suffer through rude remarks as a woman. Sexism and sexual harassment have come a long way, but it wasn't always like it is today. Even with the laws and awareness, we still see a lot of injustice for women in the workplace. Being a black woman brought another level of problems for me.

Not all of my problems stemmed from inside the office specifically, but many stemmed from outside vendors and people. I remember a vendor spoke to me rudely and was very disrespectful. My boss, without hesitation, stood up for me and told the vendor, "If you don't respect her, then we can no longer do business with you. She cuts the checks, and you need to be a little bit more nicer to her."

During the road to making more money, I had to suffer through driving a raggedy car to work. It was a mess and had to be held together with a bungee cord because someone hit me and didn't pay. Sometimes the heat wouldn't work, and we were freezing during our commute.

When my aunt kept my sons, I also would carpool with my mom to get her to work and use her car so I wouldn't be cold. More than a few times, I was at work praying that the car would crank. I would turn the key, and nothing would happen. It was like it died, and it couldn't have been at at more worse time.

It was nothing short of a miracle when my hard work paid off. When I advanced academically and corporately, the first thing I did was buy a house and a car. It felt good to get both things in my name without any help. That Mitsubishi, Galant, and house meant so much because it was part of my reminder for why I had to endure for my family.

Chapter Five

God was blessing me for enduring the pain on the back end. I can remember the day I went to the nursing home and checked out my great-grandmother Alice. I took her for a drive in my new car, and I pulled up in the driveway of my new house. I told her, "Look, Grandma, this is my new house! I bought myself a house!"

Grandma Alice says, "You bought this by yourself?" I replied, "Yep." She hugged me and told me that she was proud of me. She told me to remember to take care of the blessings God gave me, and he would give me more. She looked again at the house and said, "I am so glad God blessed you and the boys. Keep taking care of them. You are doing good."

We sat in the car for a little while longer. She was not able to walk to enter the house, but she said, finally, "I can't get out to go see it, but it's just beautiful." I knew from her reactions that she was proud of me and happy for what God had done for our family. I represented change and possibility for all of us.

That's the last ride that she and I had together. I'm really blessed because my great-grandmother got this chance to see her two great-grandkids, and they were the oldest great-grandkids that she had. I am so grateful for the time that was spent with her; never in a million years would I have thought that she would leave us shortly after. I loved great-grandmother Alice unconditionally because she was my rock. I went on to spend a lot of nights in the hospital with her, and I am glad I did. I gained so much wisdom from her.

Chapter Six

Life was filled with growth and learning curves. I achieved a lot by the time I turned twenty-five. But life would still teach me new things that I didn't sign up for. Not all the things were bad, of course, but some were really hard to accept. As we live life, it can be hard to see the people we have to leave behind for one reason or another.

My marriage was something I left behind, but my independence was something I had to gain in a positive way. I remember booking my first flight alone. The first time I took a plane was with my ex-husband, and we went to Texas when I was 19 or twenty. Now at twenty-six, I am doing my own thing and calling the shots.

I felt proud of myself on the plane, although I hated being alone. When I got on the ground, I had to decide what I wanted to do, and many of those activities were alone. I wondered, was this what life would feel like going forward?

There was a lot of death floating around me while I was trying to figure things out for myself. In February 2006, I lost Alice Ruth King, my beloved great-grandmother. In 2007, I lost my aunt Bonita Wise, and in 2008,

I lost my aunt Angela King. In 2009, I lost another grandmother, Shirley King. Also, in 2008 or 2009, my mother became partially quadriplegic because of a back surgery. In 2009, I also lost Benita's son, Marquess.

A lot of funerals kept happening between 2006 and 2010. It was hard for me because I was still grieving the death of one person when another would die. It was like when I was trying to get counseling for my father's death and the issues I had going on, I was having to talk more about loss.

I was glad to see a positive event take place in my life in 2010. I earned my master's degree in November after working tirelessly for the past few years. I was glad I spent as much time as I did with each of my grandmothers, aunts, cousins, and family growing up. It does seem like no matter how much time we have with someone, seeing them gone, the time was never enough.

Also in 2010, I had a hysterectomy due to the stress and strain on my body from helping to lift my mother and grandmother. Lifting them to help and care for them was not easy to do. At the time, I mostly cared for my mother by myself. I had no help to lift their weight, so that meant I had to lift them with any part of my body that would give me the strength.

Doing this repeatedly for months with my mother and years with my grandmother cost me physically. However, I wouldn't change a thing about taking care of those who helped me grow up. My uncle Kenny and sister Shanice took on the responsibility for my mother's care after my grandmother passed. I have always been there to assist with logistics, but I don't know what I would do without these two.

Chapter Six

I was in a relationship, a long-term one that didn't seem to progress. We were in the boyfriend, or dating phase, for a long time. He was a decent man, and I don't know why things didn't progress much. It could have been me and my many thoughts, or how busy I was, and my need to provide and take care of things. I just realized that although he was here in the physical realm, he really couldn't be there for me like I needed him or anyone to be.

I needed shoes filled in my life that no one could fill but God. I was looking for my flaws and hypercritical of my mistakes because I wanted to get everything right. I wanted to be great at everything, and missing the mark was like a boulder hitting me hard. I felt a lot of pressure and stress, and keeping all the plates spinning on sticks was a juggling act to behold. I knew that life could be delicate and no one could predict the direction.

I was about 30 years old, going through loss from death, pain from helping others who were sick, issues with owning a house, dealing with a long-term dead-end relationship, and my children were a lot. School was completed, but the need to care for my mom filled in the gap of time. I kept working and trying to help my boyfriend run a business we shared. The business was initially started by his cousin, and he passed it on to us.

When I thought life was giving me a break, many of the seniors in my family were dying, but I took comfort in the fact that my cousins and all the grandchildren had each other. I think now, as I reflect, I never cried at my father's funeral because I think that meant accepting he was dead. I was carrying a lot of weight in my heart, and being strong for everybody grew tiresome. I used to tell my best friend, and one of my very close cousins, Charles

Kelly, everything.

It hit me like a ton of bricks when he died in 2012. He was young, and we grew up together. Later that same year, Nikki was hit by a car and she also died. Another cousin and childhood friend. My circle of family and friends was getting smaller. It was like a wound opened back up larger, over and over again, similar to when I lost my dad.

I needed my boyfriend to be there for me, but he wasn't. We were on and off again for a lot of reasons. One of the main problems we had was an insecurity I didn't realize was there. It was not a supportive relationship, and he, too, was pulling on my energy and heart.

When I needed him to be there for me, he wasn't there, so I did what I did best. I leaned on God, I dug deep into counseling, and I tried to become a better version of myself regardless of whether he helped to get there. Everything felt like it was closing in around me, with seeing familiar places that reminded me of the ghosts of those passed on. I needed a fresh start and to get into a new environment, or at least I felt that way.

So, I picked up and moved out of Covington and went Hampton, GA. I was there for probably about a year, then I moved to Thornton Road. I still owned the previous house, but I rented it out. Eventually, I left Thornton Road to come back to Lithonia, Georgia. I realized no matter where I went, there was a problem, and the problem was either with me or within me. I wasn't sure of which, so I had to get quiet and alone to find out.

The relationship that was going nowhere stayed stalled. I let the separation swell and got by myself to pray

Chapter Six

about it. I said to God in a prayer, "You know, I know I messed up. I've been looking for my daddy in these folks, and I don't want what I want for me. I want what you want for me." For several years, I lost sight of that, and although God kept blessing me, I knew I needed to give him more to have more of him in my life.

When I switched my focus to be on God in every way, that's when I started to live my best life.
I had a house in Covington, but I had no plans of coming back. I was living in Lithonia, although I worked in Fairburn. I ended up selling my house in Covington because I didn't see a future for me there anymore. I had no plans of coming back to Covington. Lo and behold, a family member got in trouble and needed my help.

I was about 34 years old at this time. So I drove up from Fairburn to see about my family, and to be more specific, to get them out of jail. To get him and her out, I remembered a bail bondsman from back in the day who helped another family member. It wasn't the best time to see him again, but I was grateful to see a familiar face who helped us before.

We were cordial, and he was very professional. I enjoyed our conversation, but didn't think anything of it. I got in my car to go home, and the bondsman texted my phone. I thought I had forgotten to sign or do something, so I asked him, "Hey, did I forget something?" He joked with me and then asked me out on a date. I was a little surprised, so my response was simple, "Sure."

I laugh as I think about it now, but then I had a swell of emotions and ideas cross my mind before the date. I didn't want to get nervous or put too much pressure on things. I knew I didn't want to waste my time playing games, but I also wasn't too sure I wanted to jump into a relationship, let alone a marriage, either.

I remember telling myself, "Just breathe. It's just a date." That helped me to calm down and just let the moment be the moment. I told myself, "It is what it is." Fast forward a bit, that date turned into a relationship, which is now my current relationship.

In this relationship with the bondsman, things were going great. He made me feel loved and appreciated, but I lived far. The distance was difficult at times, and when he asked me to come and live with him, that was different for me. For the past ten years, I have been maintaining homeownership by myself. Anyone I dated, they came to live with me, and not the other way around.

It was a vulnerable position to put myself into, for sure, but for love, I agreed to take another risk. I sold everything except for some furniture to move back to Covington, the humble place of my birth. Isn't that ironic?

When it was time to move, he was different than my other experiences. He didn't lean on me or expect me to do things alone. When it was time to pack up my house and move in, he helped me pack and drive my stuff to the home we would share.

I moved into a family home with him, thinking we would buy something together when the time was right. At that time, we didn't want to get married right away. We wanted to live together for the first two years to see how it goes.

I refused to marry someone whom I didn't know. The only way to really get to know someone is to be

Chapter Six

around them all the time. Trying to get used to each other wasn't a huge challenge, but it took effort. It was my first time living in a house that I didn't actually own. With this arrangement, I had some reservations because I could be asked to leave, then where would I go? Previously, it was the other way around, and I can tell them to leave. So that made it a little bit different because I'm now in somebody else's stuff and not my own.

We looked at buying a home, but nothing seemed to fit his liking. I, too, wasn't in a hurry because I hadn't settled on a job I liked. I would take contracts to keep my schedule free for the right job to pop up. I wasn't going to settle for a permanent position somewhere I didn't like. I guess this was a running theme in my life around this time.

Around this time, I just kinda bounced around a little bit. It was when I moved back to Covington that I realized how much my mom really needed me. With my flexible schedule, I was able to be there for her more. Having a partner who was stable and supportive of me also meant I didn't have any pressure or problem with helping my mother with the stuff she needed.

I spent a lot of time with my mom and got to be closer to my kids because I didn't live away in the city. It was a blessing to have this bondsman in my life, but also kind of scary because I had never lived with somebody before. What also made this situation unique was that I took on the challenge of moving in with him and a kid that he was raising.

Before this relationship, I would settle for things in people that were not in my best interest. I was used to taking care of everybody and expecting very little in return. I wasn't an adult in thinking through what I needed because I was still struggling with my father and daddy issues. When I started this relationship, I really was in a much better place than I had ever been in before.

I was not a wounded girl trying to find love; I was a woman, mature, and confident of who I was and my value. Before, I questioned that a lot, but in this relationship, it never once took over. I kept going to counseling for years, and I have no shame in admitting that. It took me decades to be who I was, and I shouldn't expect two sessions or even a year to erase all of that. It took me time, and I am grateful for my journey and process.

I won't say that everything was behind me because I still had problems. I was still trying to let my need to compare my past go. I was still on the road to becoming a better version of myself, and I am thankful that the love of my life loved me through it. I am grateful even to my mom, who helped me through it.

I remember one occasion when I was sitting at home on the couch, pouring my eyes out. Why am I doing this? I thought as I sat there. I spent years never crying, why am I crying now? Why do I feel like a fresh wound is open, like when my dad passed away so long ago?

Why can't I just let it go? Why can't I just let my dad rest in peace, you know? The questions became stronger in my heart, and they took over my thoughts, too. I swallowed my fear one day, and I asked my mother in one of our many conversations about what I was going through. I asked her the hard questions I had asked myself, hoping to hear something I didn't know I needed.

Chapter Six

Her answer helped me to answer some of my why questions. I also understood her a bit more than I did before. She showed me how to look at people. Yes, you can see the differences, but you don't have to compare them to something you are or thought you were missing. I was missing something most of my adulthood that I couldn't get back. And so, all those deaths just kept taking a toll on me. When I cried about the loss of my father, I cried about loss across the board.

It was like everybody and everything that I loved was being snatched from me. I'm not sure if this is why I ran from marrying the man who was good to me, or not. You know? But I could see how that might have played a role.

Everything that I had for a backbone system was being snatched from me as well. I was trying to learn how to cope with it all and not make the same mistakes I did in my past. Loss made me very cautious because it showed me how fragile life can be. How sensitive and powerful our emotions could become.

I didn't want my emotions to take over my heart and mind again. I wanted to choose this life and be certain that this was what I wanted and was best for me. I wanted what God wanted for me, not what I liked or could grow to love.

All this stuff that I had been through led me to look over the bad and find the good. I was positive, but to a huge fault. I disguised reality, and that cost me big time. I didn't want another bad man in my life. Equally true, I didn't want to waste time, money, my emotions, or sense of self and respect.

I want to encourage whoever's reading this book to make sure you pick and fight your battles wisely. Don't come off of what you're doing, and don't lower your standards for people who don't mean you no good. Go with your gut and not with your emotions. Go with your heart and pray about it.

If God has given you an answer or a sign, you'd best to believe it. Don't waste time on people who ain't willing to work with you to get to the next level. If they can't build with you while you're down, then you don't need them while you're up. Don't let people disrespect you, and don't be a pushover.

Don't climb off the wall to address minor issues. Keep going and be the best version of yourself. And whatever you did, whatever your parents did, you ought to be able to be accountable for your own actions. If you are hurt by the past, you need to consider going to counseling or figure out why you are still holding on to the pain and can't let it go. Holding on to the past and holding on to those emotions is not getting you where you need to go.

You cannot move forward looking in the rear view at your past, that's keeping you blinded from what's up ahead. When I was in my late thirties, I was zeroed in on going forward and not looking behind me. I came into a new environment where I didn't have to screw in the knob. I was finally able to be a lady and let somebody try to take care of me for once. I ain't saying that I was perfect or arrived by the time I was thirty-six, but I was a lot clearer.

Going through loss sent me on an emotional roller coaster that was about to come off the track. Some days were harder than others. I can remember going to the counseling office saying, "I'm getting this, but it's not helping." I was going through the motions, but I was only interested in hearing my own heart and not implementing what I was learning. I couldn't get to the next phase of my life because I wouldn't go through the process.

Later on, I learned counseling didn't help as intended because I didn't want it to help. I didn't wanna give up the things that were familiar to me. I didn't wanna be uncomfortable to be the best version of myself. I was still scared even when I had confidence that this situation was different. I needed to trust myself and trust that I made a good decision. I was happy, and I wanted to stay this way.

I wanted to be the best version of myself and not be alone. I had to be the best version of me and invite others to love that version of me. If I could share anything with you, "Be the best version of yourself that you can be, by not allowing nobody to dim your light. Also, let those who want to love you, love you."

Chapter SEVEN

It was an adjustment to go from having my own space and living by my rules to having to be open-minded and live with others. Living with my husband wasn't a challenge in the negative sense, but an adjustment because I had never had a relationship like this.

My husband was nothing like what I knew. I knew that when we were dating, but I was reassured of it the longer I lived with him. I could see us being together for a very long time, but I wasn't quick to jump to marriage. I had done that already more than once and questioned if that was in the cards for me.

I know sometimes when you try something and it fails, you can feel like you don't want to try again. I felt that way at first, but after more than a year of getting to know my husband, he gave me such confidence in my decision to marry him.

It was never an official proposal; we just woke up one day and discussed getting married, and we had an engagement party shortly after. We were due to get married in another country the very next year, but 6 months after the engagement, we woke up one week and decided to do it prior to the 1st of the year. We still went on and had the ceremony in Jamaica. It feels like I married him 3 times.

It wasn't too bad moving back to my small town of Covington, Georgia. Growing up here was full of so many memories, and I get why people want to leave home and never come back. Sometimes we are running from something, someone, or wanting a life change. I am guilty of all three.

I had finally found a husband with the intention to marry and take care of me. He is loving, kind, thoughtful, and wise. Felix makes me happy, and I couldn't imagine a life without him and the children we share. We both had children prior to our marriage. He had three children, and I had two. We are not perfect, but we are pretty much a happy blended family.

Returning home, I did not return the way I left Covington. I came back a better version of myself and with a far better partner. Moving into the home where my husband was born and raised in wasn't awkward because his family and I are really close. Both of his parents, I got the chance to get to know them every day that I helped support them as they grew older, we grew closer.

My father-in-law and I grew close when Felix and I were dating. He was actually the first person to congratulate us after our wedding. I remember when we were on the house hunt, he said, "You don't have to go and buy a house. You could live right here. I will give you and Felix the house. Just fix that one."

We considered what he said and took his words to heart. I could see that the house had sentimental value for both my father-in-law, mother-in-law, and my husband.

Chapter Seven

This house was a house that my husband's father, Richard, was building with his own hands. He built a portion of the house before Felix was born, but after a car accident, he couldn't finish it as he wanted to. I felt as if we were living on sacred ground because there was a baptism pool in our front yard that used to belong to the church. Considering this, the home still makes me feel a sense of peace.

We started making plans for the revisions to the home, and he came to us one day and said, "Here's the deed to the house. I don't want nothing, but for you two to fix this place up while I am still living so I can see it." It was such a sweet and grand gesture. I cried as we accepted the gift that bore a sentimental value larger than the value of the home.

My mother-in-law was also just as heartwarming to be around as her husband. They had embraced me, called me their daughter, and there was nothing they hadn't done to make me feel at home. Richard passed on May 3rd of 2025. He will always have a place in my heart, and his wife, a labor of love, I will do with a joyous heart.

So yes, the home my husband and I share is an upgrade from what I grew up in. It's amazing how God can bring us full circle, like he has with my life. My husband and I remodel the home room by room. We added on additions to make this home look and feel like us. Felix's parents loved how we made the home ours and found a way to embrace it within our family.

I think we cannot be too quick to throw out the past because we think getting new is better. I am glad we wanted to keep our history alive, and pull our lives into what has had so much meaning for both of us. It's okay to reinvent a space instead of tearing everything down, too!

Life can be like that with us; not everything about you has to change, but many rooms can use some updating for you to be a better version of yourself.

Growing up, we never had pets living in the house. As a mother, I never allowed a dog or pet to live in the house; I did try it once, but was not successful. I was okay with them outside, but never in my house. I was in a bubble for what I was used to, and it took Felix to help me relax. I remember one year he bought a gift that we could not return for Christmas.

On Christmas day, my husband had purchased a 3-lb tiny little dog for me off the internet. When I saw the dog, I thought she was a teddy bear, but no, she was a breathing dog. I felt bad that I thought about returning her at first. She was only a month old and left her mom; I thought it was too soon. But my husband assured me things would be well, and he trained her for me.

My dog's name is Cookie, and she has become a great part of our family. I love this dog and wondered why I hadn't done something like this sooner, gotten an indoor pet. I liked this version of myself that wasn't too strict with how things had to be. I grew okay with shifting away from the familiar. One thing I remember learning from my parents and grandparents was washing walls.

I used to wash walls weekly because I like a clean house. I think this might have been why I didn't have animals. I thought they brought their own set of germs, cleaning, and I didn't see why adding more work on my already full plate made any sense. Funny thing, how time and people can change all of that.

My husband and I work so well, I think, too, because we are willing to support each other. I never tried to change him, but the changes we have both made to welcome a life together have made us both better. We have mutual respect for each other's careers, and this mutual respect makes us great partners.

We look forward to being empty nester's someday to see what dynamics that will bring to our lives too. We are good friends and have such a healthy connection; bringing our children together is not a challenge. Our children love both of us and have embraced our family, too. We have one son still living at home, and it was a challenge for me to live with two grown men. I must tell you that, because of the rules I normally had growing up, which I even instilled in my boys.

Men don't see the purpose in washing walls weekly. I finally got that at 37 years old. Some things about us take time for us to make changes that make us a bit softer and more understanding. I am grateful that I have not fought against my advancement. Another anchor that has helped me keep my heart towards change and growth is our church home, Good Hope Baptist Church.

This church has been in the Spring Hill community for years. It's very important to have roots wherever you call home, so you can be connected and know you have help and support. I love my church and would encourage anyone to join other clubs, groups, and organizations that can help you connect more with others. In addition to my church family, I also enjoy being involved in the Madison Women's Network Mentorship Program.

Staying connected with these ladies has helped me to develop as a professional. Some decisions I needed to make, I gained the confidence to make by being in this group. We don't always have someone in our family who can give us answers for business, career, or life. Having a group that offers women of every age and stage to help you is an invaluable resource.

What I love most about the group is although I am a mentee inside the organization. There are always more steps for you to become the best version of yourself if you are still alive. Seeing what I have had to endure over the years, how I persevered, has been a benefit for other women, too. I think sometimes we can think our story won't matter, or it doesn't need to be told. I am pleasantly surprised by the good that comes from telling my story.

I didn't have the ideal setup of having all of my children in a single relationship, or only getting married once with great success. My life has been an organic journey with my imperfections. Our day-to-day lives are a make-up of our decisions and those of others we love or have loved and care about. Yes, even those we didn't care too much for also.

But every day I get up and work eight to five, I don't mind it. I love my profession as a payroll manager. I love working with people, and the company I am employed with has been very good at helping me achieve my personal goals. I am proud of the work my husband does as a bail bondsman and how his profession provides for us and supports families.

Life isn't perfect. Time has a way of helping you accept the things you can't change and work on the things you can. I cannot change my childhood, but I can work on the relationship I want now with my mother, family, and others. I am empowered to reclaim the situations in my life that brought pain, but shifting my focus to what I care to be lasting memories.

I spend a lot of telephone time with my mother now, and I often see her, and I love it. The aunt who raised me, I spent a lot of time with her, too. She and her husband allowed me to share their room growing up, and I always wanted to do something for them. I am happy to say that she lives in a better house now. It is not only nice when you upgrade, but when your whole family can upgrade with you. The same heart that my aunt has to give her time and love, she is still doing.

She is gifted at helping people overcome their life challenges with patience and love. It is a blessing to my heart to see her happy, and everyone she is hosting has their own rooms. My uncle George was a blessing to me, too, and will be forever missed, same as my father-in-law, who both passed in 2025.

My mom also moved out of the family home in Jamestown into another place. She now has adequate living conditions with central heating and air. She has all the amenities that I have, and lives just as good as me, if not better. That's been my goal in life to make sure that I take care of the people who have taken care of me.

Everybody is doing okay. We are dealing with family members who are growing older or dealing with sickness, but no one is living in poor conditions. My great-grandmother was right about what she said about education. Education has helped us all afford the lives we live now, and I think she would be proud to see how we live now.

All my life, I have tried to become the best person I could be. I support my community, help take care of my family, and work on myself. Changing your circumstances is not just about you, but everyone else around you. Changing and making an impact also means you will need the help of others. I am grateful for the people who have helped me in life and kept me encouraged.

It is a wonderful realization to know we have completed 90% of our renovation project. We have paid off the vehicles we own, and are not at risk of financial ruin. Our children are healthy, my family is doing good, and life is a blessing. Yes, there are good and bad days, but mostly good.

I love that I work from home and can avoid Atlanta traffic. It is the simple things that we learn to appreciate as we get older. All of this started because I stopped running from getting my education. I didn't look at defeat and run in the other direction for too long. I faced the science class I failed, and it dominated my future educational plans. If you are stuck because of a GED or lack of education, don't be afraid to go back to school.

I learned that you can go back when you are determined to. When you are focused and content on giving life your best, you will find success and hope to move things forward. I cannot express how important education is. Even if you don't ever use it on a job, it's the one single thing that nobody can ever take from you.

Next, in life, relationships can succeed or fail. It doesn't matter who is to blame, but learn from your mistakes. Learn not to repeat what led you astray or sent you in a different direction than your goal. I was looking for my father and making the same mistake over and over again. I needed healing and to remember that my future was mine to decide.

Chapter Seven

I got divorced, and I had to remind myself of what I wanted. I decided to be in a relationship and to date again. I wanted to do things differently and with someone who reminded me of nothing in my past. I dated again, and if you want to date again, date. Don't let nobody determine your life.

Don't be so fearful of what can happen and if you will make mistakes. You might, but grow through them. No one is perfect, right? If you want to get with your husband and be an empty nester, do that. I think at this point in our lives, it's time for us to enjoy our lives too. I wrote this book because I believe it is important to tell your story, to remind yourself of your journey, and see how you have overcome what you faced.

This book doesn't recount everything that happened in my life, but it is just a synopsis. I don't think we can ever tell everything we have lived and experienced in one book. But what I can tell you is if you got a child and your child has experienced some kind of loss, or you, get help early on. I wish I had gotten counseling about my father and learned to grieve sooner.

I needed help to cope and process stress, and if I had done that sooner, maybe I could have relaxed more over the years or made better decisions. A lot of people are on blood pressure medication and all kinds of stuff because they're not letting their stress out or having healthy conversations about their needs. You need an outlet and relationships, clubs, church, a marriage, or a counselor can help you do that.

We all have stuff balled up from our childhood that we haven't gotten over if we didn't take the time to work through it. I encourage you to do the work to process your trauma, and don't be afraid to overcome it. The only way to be a better version of yourself is to acknowledge the version you are now.

It is my prayer that if your mental health is not where it should be, this book will encourage you to take a step forward. I have friends who I know decided to linger too long in the past. They have trauma, and that trauma, if not addressed, can lead to long-term pain. I would cry some nights looking at friends who are stuck and not living well, because they never took time out for themselves. You have to strive to be well, to heal for yourself, so you can help others. Don't let your pain linger too long or get so far gone that you feel hopeless.

Don't let it get so far gone that you feel nobody can help you. It's a hard pill to swallow when you can't get your blessing because you're dealing with something that's from the past, and you can't look forward. If someone is causing your mental peace, I encourage you to take time for yourself. Just because you have children with someone doesn't mean they are your family. It doesn't mean that they have to be in your life the rest of your life in the same way.

For relationships you left, you left that relationship for a reason. Stop looking in the past and look to the future because as long as you keep looking at the past relationship with your child, mama, daddy, or any lingering person, the longer it will take you to see what's ahead. You will only block yourself from your blessing by focusing on your pain or disappointments. Move forward with your life in all aspects and stop holding your parents accountable for your actions.

I had to let go of the blame I had against my father

for the poor decisions I was making in my life. We can blame our poor decisions on our upbringing or the things we lack, but ultimately, at what age do we start holding ourselves accountable? We need to be accountable for our own actions. We need to move forward with life and be the best human beings we can be. God blesses those who help themselves and others.

I had help and helped others, not even knowing why I was helping. I wanted nothing in return, but God has turned things around and made things happen for me that I would have never believed would happen. Sometimes I wonder why it happened for me–Why has God been so good to me? All I can say is, "God, thank you," as I look back on my life. "The storm is over, and you blessed me to reach the other side of the storm."

I'm grateful for this life, and I'm grateful for everything that I've went through because it has helped me to be the strong person I am today. I've been bent over like a palm tree, but I didn't break because I knew where my health and strength come from. It comes from God. He's always been here, and is still here with me.

I remember before I started this journey, I was in the dental office. For the first time ever, I underwent anesthesia using laughing gas. I remember being so light, and it felt funny. The laughing gas made me so relaxed. And I was like, "Lord, I ain't ready to go yet because I got to tell my story." My father-in-law was the first to tell me to do it. My uncle George was supportive and was alive during the time of the production of this book, too.

At the time, I didn't know why I said this or where it was coming from. It could have been my subconscious or God speaking through me, I am not sure, but God said, "Go out there and tell your story. Tell people that I do exist." Don't be afraid of life because we all came here and we all got to go. NO one stays here forever, but we all get to choose the legacy we leave here.

We get to choose our legacy and mark on the world. The dates between the dashes, choose to make them all count. When I leave from here, I want God to have his hands open to me and say, "Good Job; well done. You've done what I asked you to do. Now come on and take your rest." Like so many of my family have done before me.

God is always here to help you through your pain. Don't be afraid to take his help and share your story. I wasn't afraid, and I am so glad that I was not.

About the Author

As an expert in financial solutions, Mrs. Johnson boasts a distinguished career spanning over two decades. She currently serves as the co-owner and chief financial officer of Coflex Solutions Inc., a position she has held since 2014. In this role, she has demonstrated exceptional leadership and financial acumen, contributing significantly to the company's growth and success. Her expertise in problem-solving has been instrumental in navigating complex financial landscapes, earning her recognition within the industry.

In addition to her role at Coflex Solutions, Mrs. Johnson has been the payroll manager at Filtration Group's Porex Corporation since 2017. Her responsibilities include overseeing payroll operations and ensuring compliance with financial regulations. Her commitment to excellence is further exemplified by her active membership in the Madison Women Network Mentorship Program, where she engages with other professionals to foster growth and development within her field.

Mrs. Johnson's academic journey laid a strong foundation for her professional achievements, earning a Master of Business Administration in accounting and finance from the American Intercontinental University Online in 2010. This accomplishment is particularly significant as she overcame challenges as a single mother of two children to achieve her educational goals.

In addition to her academic credentials, Mrs. Johnson is a certified notary public. Reflecting on her career, she attributes much of her success to her problem-solving abilities and organizational skills, which have consistently guided her through various challenges and opportunities throughout her career.

Outside of her professional life, Mrs. Johnson is deeply committed to her family, enjoying spending time with her husband and both her biological and stepchildren. Additionally, she enjoys volunteering in her community in her free time.

SCAN ME

**Call or Text:
770-240-0089 Press Extension 1
Web: KLEpub.com
Email Services@klepub.com**

It's time to start and finish **YOUR Story!**

KLE Publishing specializes in helping people become authors. In as little as 15 to 90 days, we can help you develop your books and e-books and publish to 39,000 outlets! We also offer audiobook services.

Write, Edit, Format, Publish
We can help from
Start to Finish.

Explore and learn more about published authors affiliated with KLE.

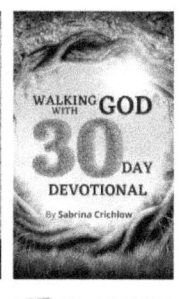

KLEPub.com

www.ingramcontent.com/pod-product-compliance
Lightning Source LLC
Chambersburg PA
CBHW050040080526
44586CB00014B/1382